GET READY FOR WORK

A Career Preparation Workbook for Legal Students

SHARYN BOROVOY

2010
EMOND MONTGOMERY PUBLICATIONS
TORONTO, CANADA

Emond Montgomery Publications Limited
60 Shaftesbury Avenue
Toronto ON M4T 1A3
http://www.emp.ca/college

Printed in Canada.
Reprinted August 2011.

We acknowledge the financial support of the Government of Canada through the Canada Book Fund for our publishing activities.

To my family, Ted, Kylie, Jason, Lisa, Daniel, little Josh, and Nanci.

Acquisitions and development editor: Peggy Buchan
Marketing manager: Christine Davidson
Director, sales and marketing, higher education: Kevin Smulan
Supervising editor: Jim Lyons
Copy editor: Geraldine Kikuta
Proofreader: Francine Geraci
Text and cover designer and typesetter: Shani Sohn

Library and Archives Canada Cataloguing in Publication

Borovoy, Sharyn

Getting ready for work : a career preparation workbook for legal students / Sharyn Borovoy.

ISBN 978-1-55239-365-9

1. Law students—Vocational guidance—Canada. 2. Law students—Employment—Canada. 3. Résumés (Employment)—Handbooks, manuals, etc. 4. Employment interviewing—Handbooks, manuals, etc. 5. Job hunting—Canada—Handbooks, manuals, etc. I. Title.

KE330.B67 2010   340.023'71   C2009-906907-5
KF297.B67 2010

Table of Contents

Introduction

Congratulations! You are ready to embark on your career as a law clerk or legal assistant. But what happens now? Your work experience may have been in a very different field, such as retail or customer service. Perhaps you have never been on a formal job interview. You might be looking at changing jobs. Whatever stage you are at, preparing for a job interview that can lead to the next chapter in your life can be very stressful.

The purpose of this workbook is to help you obtain employment and start a career in your chosen field. It assumes that you have found a job posting or advertisement for a job in law that interests you. This book is designed to assist you in doing what needs to be done to get an interview for the position, and then to prepare you to be successful.

The competition for a job in today's market can be fierce. A great deal of planning needs to go into the job search process before you even get to the interview stage. You need to put your best foot forward and make the best impression possible for a potential employer. How do you accomplish that? This workbook will take you through the necessary steps.

As you work through the exercises, you will learn the answers to the following questions:

- What do I have to do before I get an interview?
- How do I present myself in a professional manner?
- What is important and needs to be discussed in a job interview?
- What kind of questions will I be asked?
- What questions should I ask a potential employer about the firm? about the job? about my chances for advancement?
- What questions should not be asked in an initial interview?
- What should I wear?
- How do I greet the people at the interview?
- What time should I get there?
- What should I do to follow up after the interview?
- What are some of the important things I should do and should never do?

On a larger scale, how do I present myself as the polished professional career person who is "right for this job"?

This practical workbook will force you to think about things that you might not have considered before. It will take you through the interview process step by step. It will assist you in preparing your own questions and answers in an intelligent and thoughtful way. The goal of this workbook is to act as an important tool that will result in a successful job interview and legal career.

CHAPTER 1

The Resumé and Covering Letter

The Purpose of the Resumé

A resumé is designed to present yourself and your accomplishments in a professional and organized manner. It is a tool that will enable you to showcase your education, experience, and abilities in such a way that an employer will want to hire you. Your resumé could be the deciding factor in whether or not a potential employer would like to offer you an interview. It introduces you before you ever take a step inside the interview room. As a result, you want your resumé to demonstrate that you are professional, qualified, and ready for the challenge of this new opportunity.

Many large law firms receive hundreds of resumés per week. Most resumés receive a brief glance before a decision is made as to whether to move on to the next stage or not. How will you make your resumé stand out?

Use features that will catch the employers' eye while at the same time are substantive. Use word features you have learned. Use bolding, bullets, tables, centring, and different font styles and sizes. Show what you can do. Be careful not to be too flashy, though, or your resumé will lose the professional image you are striving to achieve.

There are many different styles of resumés and you should prepare different resumés for different positions that you are applying for. If your college offers a co-op or field placement, you might also have a different style of resumé for that purpose. The focus of this chapter will be on a resumé for someone coming out of a legal program in a college who has no related full-time work experience.

Your resumé should always look professional. This is the first sample of your work that a potential employer will see. The resumé should highlight both your academic and work-related accomplishments. The format should be easy to read, starting with your most recent job experience or academic achievements and working backward in time. At this early stage in your career, your resumé should not be longer than two pages, not including your references, which should be on a third, separate page. Potential employers will disregard resumés that go on and on. Never include a picture.

It is absolutely essential that your resumé be totally free of errors. If there are any spelling errors or typos, most law firms will throw it in the recycling bin without even reading it. Most potential employers think that, if an applicant cannot put the proper amount of time and effort into something as important as a resumé, the quality of his or her work in the workplace will be equally poor. Do not waste their time and yours. If you want to work in the area of law, your work cannot just be good. It must be perfect!

Make your resumé an excellent example of your work. Take the appropriate time and effort to ensure that it is professional and perfect to help you get a foot in the door of the job of your dreams.

Content of the Resumé

Letterhead

Personalize the letterhead for your resumé, starting with your name in boldface and in a larger font so that it stands out. Next, set out your mailing address, including your full street address and postal code. Then, set out all of your current contact information including a telephone number and email address. If you include two telephone numbers, indicate which one is a residential number and which is a cellphone number so that there is no confusion. Make sure that you have a professional message on your phones, because you never know when a potential employer may be calling. This is not the time for a "cool" phone message on your answering machine. Also make sure that you have created a professional email address to use strictly for your resumé. Use your school email or open a Gmail account or a new account that has your first and last name, if possible, because that is considered more professional and appropriate.

Objective Statement

If you are looking for a full-time position, you may choose to include an objective statement on your resumé. However, it is not always necessary. When you do include one, always keep it specific to the job and profession you are seeking. The key is to keep your objective statement short and sharp.

Education

If your resumé is for your first full-time legal job or for field placement, show your education and your academic achievements first. Give complete information about each educational program by naming the school, the program, and some details of this program as it relates to the job or field placement position you are hoping to acquire. Include the dates (month/year) for each school attended.

Start with the current program and highlight the parts of the program that are relevant for the job or placement. In other words, indicate which segments of your training and experience will help you contribute positively to this organization. Highlight skills from your experience that will relate to a potential position. Always ask yourself "What can I do for them?" *not* "What can they do for me?"

Next, state any diplomas or degrees from other post-secondary institutions. Again, list the name of the school in full and the program. Give details of degrees and/or diplomas received.

Remember to keep the formatting uniform throughout this and every other section of your resumé. Dates should line up in the same place and format throughout. Set out the month and year when you started the program and the date you finished. Use bullets and point form rather than sentences. Remember that no punctuation is necessary at the end of each bullet.

Work Experience

Start with your most recent work experience and move backward in time. Show the dates worked (from and to) together with the full name of the organization. Include your job title. Use bullets instead of sentences when describing job duties. Never use the word "I" in your resumé. Use action words when discussing job duties.

Here is a list of verbs you might use on your resumé to describe your duties on a previous job:

- arranged
- developed
- composed
- coordinated
- organized
- prepared
- improved
- supervised
- collaborated

- drafted
- edited
- facilitated
- assisted
- compiled
- collected
- reviewed
- demonstrated
- implemented

Use several of these verbs to describe the duties of your most recent job:

_____

_____

_____

_____

_____

Never exaggerate or try to make yourself or your job sound more important than it is. Always be honest.

If a job was part time and does not relate to your full-time goals, keep the details brief with only one or two bullets per job. If your work duties were similar to those in the type of job you are applying for, give more details. Make sure you emphasize any transferable duties or skills that could be used in the position you are applying for.

Computer Skills

It is a good idea to list your computer skills and the different types of software that you have been exposed to during your program of study. With so much use of technology in law firms today, your technical knowledge and skills might set you apart from other candidates. Keep working on the computer skills learned in classes you have taken. Use the word formatting skills and the word shortcut skills you have learned.

It is essential to constantly be working on improving your keyboarding skills and increasing your speed. The faster and more accurately you are able to keyboard, the quicker you will be able to finish your work, and you will be more of an asset to the firm. The importance of fast, accurate keyboarding skills cannot be stressed enough. Keep practising your keyboarding! The more rapidly you can complete the work, the better for you. Remember that quality must *never* suffer. Always push yourself to strive for excellence!

Think about the different software programs you have learned in class and the different areas of law where the various programs are used. You probably will surprise yourself at the number of different software programs you have learned and used that you will be able to list on your resumé.

List the different software programs you know how to use:

_____

_____

_____

_____

_____

Scholarships and Awards

It is always a good idea to highlight your accomplishments. If you have received any awards or scholarships, set out the details together with the date received. Again, start with the most current and work back in time.

Volunteer Experience

Remember, law firms are very community-minded. Sometimes having volunteered might set you apart from another candidate who is equally as qualified but has not done any volunteer work.

If you have not done any volunteer work, do not include this heading in your resumé but consider doing some in the near future.

Professional Associations/Affiliations

If you are a member of any professional associations, set them out here. These memberships say something about your mindset. They say that you are a person who gets involved, is willing to do something outside of the job after hours, and that you want to learn more and make a contribution.

If you are not a member of any associations, do not include this in your resumé but consider becoming a member soon.

Other Languages

In today's market there are so many firms that request fluency in other languages because so much of law takes place on a global playing field, working with people from all over the world. Being able to communicate in other languages can be a strong advantage for the firm and for you. This could also set you apart from other applicants. It is therefore important to indicate if you speak any other languages. Always note on your resumé other languages that you can read or write fluently.

Hobbies and Interests

It is not expected nor is it recommended that hobbies and interests be listed. If you have some interests or hobbies that are unique to you and wish to list them, keep them to a minimum. We all love to read and travel.

References

Before you apply for a job, contact three people you would like to use as references on your resumé and ask their permission to do so. If you are graduating from college, one of these people should be a professor or instructor in your program of study. Include all details for each person such as full name and job title, complete address, including postal code, and phone number. Do *not* say "References Available upon Request."

You can use the sample resumé on the following page as a template. Please note that this resumé is for people coming out of college with no full-time legal work experience. Education is highlighted and shown first on this resumé.

If you do have full-time legal work experience, show Work Experience first, starting with your current or most recent employment. The section for Education would then follow.

STUDENT NAME
1760 Finch Avenue East,
Apt 1777
North York, Ontario M2J 5G3
Residence Telephone: (416) 491-0000 ext 000
Cell: (416) 898-7458
Email: sname@learn.senecac.on.ca

Education

Sept. 20__ – present   Law Clerk Accelerated (Diploma) Program
                            Seneca College of Applied Arts and
                            Technology

This program trains students to work under the supervision of a lawyer in
a legal, governmental, or corporate office. The curriculum, which is
practice-based, covers a wide range of subjects, including real estate,
corporate/commercial law, family law, and litigation. There is also a strong
emphasis on legal research and information technology. Every subject
focuses on practical knowledge and skills. Students must have strong
critical, analytical, and communication skills to be successful in the
program.

Sept. 2005 – April 2009   Honours B.A.—English & Cultural Studies
                            McMaster University

Work Experience

Jan. 2009 – present   Legal Assistant (Part-time position)
                            Wiley, Riley, & Smiley
                            Barristers and Solicitors
• Prepared affidavit of documents, trial records, and authorizations
• Drafted statements of claim
• Composed and edited correspondence to clients
• Organized filing system
• Supervised part-time receptionist

Sept. 2008 – Dec. 2008   Sales Associate
                            Holt Renfrew
• Developed strong customer service skills as personal shopper

July 2008 – Sept. 2008   Camp Counsellor
                            Happy Child Care
- Provided care and supervision for 12 children
- Created and delivered special event activities for campers
- Interacted with and provided daily updates to parents

April 2007 – Sept. 2007   Receptionist/Secretary
                            Olsen & Associates
- Interpersonal contact with clients on the phone and in person
- Composed correspondence and email to clients

Computer Skills
- 2007 Microsoft Office
- Teraview
- Conveyancer®
- DIVORCEmate
- PC Law™
- estate-a-base
- Fast Company

Scholarships/Awards
- President's Honour List—Seneca College (2009–2010)
- Legal Program Award Bursary (2009)

Keyboarding
- Keyboarding speed of 70 words per minute

Professional Associations/Affiliations
- Student Member of ILCO
- Member of Legal Student Studies Association (LSSA)

Volunteer Activities
- OJEN Justice Education Symposium—worked at registration desk (2009)
- Law Clerk Career Prep Day—performed various tasks to ensure day ran smoothly (2009)
- Criminal Lawyers' Fall Conference—worked at registration desk (2009)

Resumé Tips

- Make sure your resumé contact information is up to date
- Create a personal letterhead for your resumé
- Include your name, mailing address including postal code, phone numbers, and email address
- Indicate if the phone numbers given are residential or cellphone numbers
- Ensure that your cellphone message is professional and businesslike when expecting employers to call
- Ask anyone who takes a message for you to write down the caller's name and phone number and to not share personal information as to your whereabouts
- Make sure there are appropriate page breaks in the sections of the resumé
- Take the time to research the correct name and title of the HR person or manager that the resumé should be sent to and be sure to spell it correctly
- Make sure your email address is professional, *not* your fun, social email such as "partygirl@hotmail.com"
- Create a professional email address using your school account or Gmail address
- Make sure your resumé has been proofread for typos and spelling errors—resumés with mistakes are thrown in the garbage and not even read
- Have someone else proofread your resumé—mistakes in a resumé tell potential employers that you do not pay attention to detail—another pair of eyes can pick up missed errors
- Resumés should be no longer than two pages (three including References)
- Have a proper page two header with your name—Resumé on the top line and the page number on the second line to give your resumé a professional look
- A separate third page should list three references including one professor, if you are just finishing school
- Reference information should be complete including the full name, address, phone number, job title of each reference
- Resumés should be uniform in format and layout

- Resumés should start with the most recent education and job information and work backward in time
- Provide more details of job-related duties if they are related to the position that you are applying for
- Have separate subheadings for each section of the resumé
- Include any volunteer activities, especially those relevant to the job or placement
- Include all professional organizations that you belong to
- If attaching your resumé to an email, make sure that it is in the proper version so that formatting will not be lost
- Do not use your Hotmail account on your resumé—some firms throw resumés out when they see this
- Do not include hobbies such as reading, travelling, or walking on the beach
- Do not show "References Available upon Request"
- Do not use "I" in a resumé, such as "I organized the filing system and I drafted documents for court"; Instead use bullets for each duty as follows:
  - Organized filing system
  - Drafted documents for court
- Do not embellish your duties in an effort to try to make yourself or the job sound more important than it is

Resumé Tips—Exercise

Create your own list of resumé tips.

Do

_____

_____

_____

_____

_____

_____

_____

_____

Do not

_____

_____

_____

_____

_____

_____

_____

_____

Notes

_____

_____

_____

_____

Writing the Covering Letter

A covering letter should always accompany your resumé. Use the same letterhead for your covering letter that you used for your resumé. Make sure that your covering letter has proper business/legal letter formatting with regard to:

- Date line
- Inside address
- Salutation line
- Body of the letter
- Signature block

Use full block or semi-block letter style and 12-point font. Keep your letter short and be succinct in what you are saying. It should be no more than one page in length.

Covering Letter Tips

Here are some important tips when writing your cover letter:

1. Always send your covering letter to a named individual, never to "To whom it may concern." Take extra time to research who the hiring partner or HR person is so that the letter is addressed to the correct party. Make sure that you spell the names correctly.

2. Your re line should be short—one line, if possible—and it should clearly state what the letter is about.

3. Do not have a generic covering letter for all jobs. Create a new covering letter for each position that you are applying for. While it is more work, it is important to take the extra time and effort to tailor each letter for the job.

4. Your covering letter should be no longer than three or four paragraphs.

5. Always proofread your letter at least three times prior to sending it.

6. Remember to include your name at the bottom of the letter.

7. Sign your covering letter. If you are sending your letter electronically, it is acceptable to only type your name.

8. If you state in your letter that you are enclosing or attaching your resumé, make sure you include the appropriate notation after the signature block.

See the following sample covering letter.

STUDENT NAME
1760 Finch Avenue East,
Apt. 1777
North York, Ontario M2J 5G3
Residence Telephone: (416) 491-0000 ext 000
Cell: (416) 898-7458
Email: sname@learn.senecac.on.ca

Today's Date

Ms. Sally Johnson
Recruitment Specialist
Wylie, Riley, & Smiley
Barristers and Solicitors
390 Bay Street
Toronto, ON
M5R 3L3

Dear Ms. Johnson:

Re: Position for Real Estate Law Clerk

The first paragraph should express your interest in the position that is available with the firm.

The second paragraph should highlight your strengths and skills. Try to marry your skills and strengths with what they are looking for in this position. Do not exaggerate what you have done or what you are capable of doing.

The third paragraph is where you state that you are looking forward to an opportunity to discuss the position with them further. Thank them for taking the time to consider your resumé for the position.

Yours truly,

Your Name

Important Things to Consider

Always keep an open mind. Push yourself outside of your comfort zone. Think outside of the box in a few key areas. The first area is with regard to the location of the firm or place of business. Downtown may be more trouble for you to get to than an office around the corner from where you live, but there may be opportunities downtown that you are unaware of. The salary might also be slightly higher downtown than in the suburbs. Downtown, there is a whole other world going on in law that is very exciting. Do not limit your opportunities for fear of travelling. The important thing is not how long it takes to get there. What is most important is what happens once you *are* there!

It is also important to keep an open mind about the areas of law. Avoid getting your heart set on only one particular area. Do not decide that you only want a job in family law and will not look at anything else. Be open to other areas. Try new things. You might be pleasantly surprised and love an area of law that you did not consider previously.

Consider accepting a contract if a full-time position is not available. Many large firms only offer three- or six-month contracts for new employees. Be open to this. This is a great way for you and the firm to get to know each other. It is also a great way to dabble in different areas of law and meet different people within the firm. You might be a floater to start out. Seize this opportunity. Learn as much as you can. Show them that you are friendly, have a strong work ethic, and are willing to do your best on any task that you are given.

Use this space for notes on covering letters. Other important tips on covering letters are:

CHAPTER 2

Preparing for the Interview

The Purpose of the Interview

The interview is an opportunity to make a face-to-face connection with a potential employer and sell yourself. At the same time, it is a chance to meet the people who work there and see if the people and the environment are a good match for you. Are you feeling a certain connection or comfort level with the people you are meeting or the surroundings in general? Can you see yourself working there?

Treat the preparation for your interview the same way you would prepare for an exam. There are many things that need to be done prior to your interview. Do not leave them to the last minute. Be organized. Make lists of things to do. Make notes of things you would like to ask or say. Interviews can be stressful. If you are organized, it will help to relieve some of that stress. Being prepared can also mean the difference between getting the job or not.

Research

Always research the firm prior to the interview. Most firms have websites. Find out the names of the partners/lawyers and what kind of law they practise. Investigate the culture, the history, and the reputation of the firm.

Find out if there are any well-known cases handled by the firm or if one of the senior partners was recently called to the bench. You can also find out if the firm is a national or an international organization and where other offices are located. Take the time to develop a solid knowledge base about the firm. If it is a family law firm, find out if there have been any recent changes in family law. If so, be prepared to discuss them.

Research Notes

List any important things you found out about the firm from your research:

Legal Websites of Interest

Because you want to work in the legal profession, it is important to know who the players are and what is happening in law and in the legal community. There are many established organizations that are well known and committed to making a difference. It is important to be aware of them and be familiar with the contributions that they make.

The following are some suggested important legal organizations that you may wish to research prior to any interviews. A more comprehensive list can be found later in this workbook.

- The law firm that is interviewing you
- Law Society of Upper Canada (LSUC)
- Criminal Lawyers Association (CLA)
- Canadian Civil Liberties Association (CCLA)
- Institute of Law Clerks of Ontario Association (ILCO)
- Ontario Justice Education Network (OJEN)
- Association in Defence of the Wrongly Convicted (AIDWYC)

List any other important legal organizations that should be researched:

_____

_____

_____

_____

_____

_____

_____

_____

_____

_____

The Practice Interview

Going to an interview may be a new experience for you. Interviews can make you nervous because you want to put your best foot forward. If you want to become good at a skill like playing the piano, you practise. The same thing applies to going on interviews. The more you do it, the more comfortable you will be with the process. Remember, being interviewed for a law firm is a very different experience from being interviewed for a part-time job.

Hold mock interview sessions. Use a relative or friend as the interviewer and go through the steps. Open the door, enter the room, and greet the interviewer with a handshake and a warm smile. Ask your friend to ask you some common questions and some surprise questions. Practise your answers. Listen carefully to the question. Keep yourself focused on answering the question that is asked. Be clear and concise with your responses. Do not ramble with an answer that goes off in many different directions. Stay focused.

A mistake often made is to concentrate on giving answers you think the interviewer wants to hear rather than answers you are comfortable with. It is important to be your best self, not someone you think the interviewer wants you to be. Your best self is the self who has done your homework and can go in feeling confident and assured.

The Practice Run

Suppose the firm is located downtown and you live in the suburbs. Your interview is for 10:00 a.m. on Wednesday. How long will it take you to get there by public transit? How far is the closest stop? How long will it take you to walk to the firm's location? These are all important questions that require consideration. You never want to be running late for an interview. You want to be there early but not too early. How do you plan this? There is nothing worse than knowing that you will be late and running from the transit stop, trying to find the correct address to realize that you have been heading in the opposite direction.

You always want to arrive at the interview early and as calm as possible. How do you do this? Take a trip to the interview location a few days ahead of time. Find out where the office is, if there is parking or transit stops nearby. Find out how long it will take you to get to the office. Find out how long the trip will take from home. Always give yourself more time than you need to get to the interview, allowing for bad weather, heavy traffic, and unexpected delays. Check out a nearby coffee shop so that if you arrive 30 minutes before the interview, you can go there before to calm your nerves and organize your thoughts.

How early should you arrive for the interview? Arrive no more than 10 minutes prior to the interview time. The person you are meeting is very busy. Time is money. Always be punctual but coming too early is almost as bad as arriving late. The night before the interview, try to get a good night's sleep so that you will look awake and alert at the interview.

List here the name and address of the firm you are going to for your interview. Include any other important details about the location such as the main intersection, the name of the person interviewing you, and his or her phone number:

Dressing for the Interview

The importance of dressing in business attire for the interview cannot be emphasized enough. First impressions do count. From the moment a potential employer meets you, you want that person to view you as professional and capable. Your image and attitude will convey this message. Some suggest you develop a mindset as if you are already in the position.

Law firms are traditionally conservative. Dress in a professional and conservative manner. This is not the time to make a fashion statement with a funky new outfit. Choose basic colours such as navy, black, or brown. You do not need to spend a lot of money on an interview outfit to impress. Make sure that your clothes are clean and ironed and that there are no missing buttons. Have your clothes ready the night before and try them on to make sure everything fits and looks good.

Men should wear a suit or dark trousers with a shirt and tie. Polish and shine your shoes. People notice shoes. Women should wear a suit or a skirt and blouse. Some firms do not like open-toed shoes. Be aware of that when selecting your shoes for the interview. If you are wearing stockings, make sure there are no runs. If you are wearing jewellery, keep it conservative and to a minimum. The same goes for perfume or cologne. With so many people having allergies to scents, you may wish to eliminate perfume or cologne altogether. Also make sure that your hair is clean and that your makeup is at a minimum.

Cover any tattoos. If you have piercings other than in your ears, remove the rings or studs so that they are not so obvious. You might like a little jewel in your nose. A conservative law firm may not feel that is an added feature for the image of one of their employees.

Perhaps your interview is during Casual Friday and everyone is wearing jeans. You are not yet a part of the firm. You have not earned the right to dress down. Make sure you are dressed in a professional, businesslike manner. Dress for the impression that you wish to make.

Once you are part of the team, you will have an opportunity to observe how others in your position and higher positions, such as managers and partners, dress. Always dress for the position that you *want* to attain, not necessarily the one you have. If your goal is to become a manager of law clerks, start dressing like one. Remember, dressing like the professional you want to be will help to encourage confidence that others will have in your ability to do a professional job.

Notes on Preparing for the Interview

Organizing Your Questions to Ask and Answer

Before you even walk into an interview room, you need to think about what you are going to say. The answers that you give can make the difference between getting the job and being overlooked in favour of another candidate. Of course, you can never anticipate all of the questions that you will be asked. However, if you systematically think about some of those questions and the answers that you plan to give, it will help relieve some stress and nervousness. It will also provide a framework for the questions that you would like to ask the interviewer. Organizing those questions and answers is a very important step in preparing you for a successful interview.

Questions to Ask

Most interviewers often end an interview by asking if you have any questions. It is a good idea to prepare questions ahead of time. From your research on the firm's website, you should be able to put together several thoughtful, intelligent questions that reflect your research on the firm. Try to word them in an intelligent way that shows you are interested in a life with the firm. Here's an example: "From my research, I noticed that your firm is international, with offices in many countries around the world. Does your firm transfer employees to international offices?"

The interview is your opportunity to get answers to any questions that you may have. It is also a time to showcase your own achievements. We will discuss more about that a little later in the workbook.

Many of your questions might be answered throughout the interview as things are explained to you. Some examples of questions you might ask include:

> Does the firm promote from within? If it is a large firm, does everyone start off in a typing pool, working for different departments, as there is a need? How long would you stay at an entry-level position before moving on? Does the firm hire new graduates as law clerks? If not, what kind of time frame and experiences are necessary to be promoted to law clerk? What is the path or process to being promoted to law clerk? How many lawyers does each law clerk work for? Are things done on a "team" basis or is the work done independently?

There are certain questions that should not be asked in the initial interview. *Never* ask a question about salary, raises, or vacation in the first interview! If the firm is interested in hiring you, those issues will be addressed in good time.

Think of 10 questions that can be asked in an interview. List them here:

Always remember that it is never what the firm can do for *you*. It is all about what *you* can bring to the firm. What do you bring to the table? What skills, knowledge, and attributes will you contribute? What sets you apart from others who are being interviewed? Why should they hire you?

Questions to Answer

Keep in mind that the purpose of the interview is for the interviewer to get to know you. Allow that to happen. It is understandable that you might be nervous. Avoid answering questions with one-word answers. Always elaborate and explain. Allow the interviewer to see who you are. It is always important to *listen* to the question. What are you being asked? Be precise in your answer.

Remember to *answer* the question. Do not dance around it. Do not go off on a tangent and get away from the topic. Do not keep talking. Answer the question *that was asked*. Stop talking when you have done that. Speak with confidence in your answers.

It is important to plan ahead. Think of possible questions that you might be asked in an interview and decide how you would answer them. Practise your answers in front of a mirror at home so that you see what you look like.

If there are high-profile court cases in the news, read about them so that you can discuss the issues intelligently. Be prepared to discuss any recent changes in the law.

There comes a time in every interview when you are asked that dreaded question, "What are your strengths and weaknesses?" Think about your answers before the interview. Where do you plan to be in five years? Think about your goals and where you would like to be and what you would like to be doing. Be realistic in setting your goals. Show that you have thought about this and you have plans for your future. It is important to be goal-oriented and to show that you want to move forward and ahead in time. This is discussed in more detail later.

Then there is that favourite question of all time, "Why should we hire you?" You might feel that a question like that puts you on the spot and you would be right. It is meant to do just that. Here is where you should highlight your skills, accomplishments, and ambitions. Here is where you emphasize what you bring to the table. Here is where you highlight what *you* can do for *them*!

Why should they hire you? Do you have superior keyboarding skills? Do you pay particular attention to detail? Are you prepared to go the extra mile? Are you a quick study who can hit the ground running? Have you done volunteer work to feed the homeless or help the needy? Have you volunteered on committees that worked on special legal events? If not, you may want to take the time now and get involved. Lawyers and law firms are very community-minded.

In the space below, write 10 possible questions, together with appropriate answers, that you might be asked in an interview.

_____

_____

_____

_____

_____

_____

_____

_____

Strengths and Weaknesses

Think about your strong areas. What do you excel at? This is often a very difficult area for many people. They feel shy or they feel like they are bragging when asked about their strengths.

Being asked about one's strengths and weaknesses can often make you uncomfortable. Be prepared with your answers ahead of time so that you will feel cool and calm when faced with this question. It is very frustrating for an interviewer to sit and wait while the applicant tries to think about what things he or she is good at and where improvement is needed. After all, you are talking about *you*.

Think about the skills you have learned in school and at any part-time jobs. Are there any transferable skills that can be applied to a law office? If so, what are they? Think about your own unique situation. Do you speak other languages? If so, that is something that will also set you apart from other applicants. The ability to communicate in different languages is very important. Many people get jobs because of the needed languages that they speak.

If your strengths are not up to par, *work* on them! If you are keyboarding at only 40 words per minute with 5 errors, keep working on increasing your speed and decreasing your error rate. Keep pushing yourself for speed and accuracy. Remember, this is law. Your work cannot just be good. Your work *must* be perfect. You will constantly be working under deadlines. The faster you can produce the work, the better. The fewer corrections that you have to make, the faster you will complete what you have to do.

Think about yourself and what you are good at doing. Do not feel that you are bragging by answering a question about your strengths. Answer with enthusiasm and commitment. Be proud of what you can do and of what you have to offer. Some people advise that you should answer questions as if you were already in the job. Try this. See if it is comfortable for you.

Here are a few suggestions to get you thinking about any important strengths that you have to offer:

- Do you work well independently?
- Do you work well as a team player?
- Do you pay close attention to detail?
- Do you proofread each document or page at least three times before being satisfied that it is correct?
- Do you manage your time well?
- Do you know how to prioritize?
- Can you multitask?
- Are you pleasant to deal with?
- Do you enjoy interaction with others?
- Do you have good keyboarding skills?
- Do you have good telephone manners?
- Do you have good people skills?
- Are you hard working?
- Are you willing to stay until the task has been completed?
- Can you work under pressure?
- Can you meet deadlines?
- Are you focused on the task at hand?
- Do you want to do the best possible job you can?
- Do you speak more than one language?
- Are you punctual?

In the space provided on the next page, record at least 10 of your strengths that will help get you the job you want. Use strengths that best describe you. Try not to use only ideas from the above list.

Discuss your strengths here. Show a minimum of 10:

_____

_____

_____

_____

_____

_____

_____

_____

_____

_____

_____

_____

_____

_____

_____

_____

_____

_____

_____

_____

_____

_____

The discussion of your weaknesses or areas that need improvement is more difficult. You want to be honest about your weak areas. However, you do not want your weaknesses to be so serious that they will keep you from getting the position.

Perhaps you think it is okay to be a poor speller. That will never do in law because the work must be perfect. Every name and word must be spelled correctly. Every "t" must be crossed and every "i" dotted.

So what do you say when you are asked about your weaknesses? Here's one suggestion. Take what you consider to be a strength and spin it into a weakness. For example, if you are a dedicated, hard worker who always tries to complete all tasks before leaving for the day, even if that means persevering until long after everyone else has left, you might mention that this sometimes this makes you miss family functions or social events with your friends.

Another suggestion is that once you have identified an area in which you need to improve, start to do something about it. This allows you to state that you are currently taking a course in time management as you would like to have more effective skills in this area. This has taken a negative and turned it into a positive because you are taking action and steps to improve yourself in this area.

Whatever you decide to say, take the situation and turn it around so that you put a positive spin on it. You are aware of your weaknesses and you have taken steps to correct them. Remember to be honest about whatever you are saying. Do not say that you do not know or that you don't really have any weaknesses. Everyone has areas that can be improved.

Think about a couple of weaknesses that you might discuss in an interview. Describe how you can talk about them in a positive way and how you are going about improving yourself in that area. Use the space provided below:

Organizing Your Skills

You already possess many skills. Some, you may take for granted. Others you might not even be aware that you demonstrate. Think about the things that you have done in the past in full-time and part-time jobs. Think about the job description. Think about the skills that you have learned in school throughout the years. What are some skills you find come easy? Some of these skills will be hard skills. Some will be soft skills. Some of your skills will be transferable from the classroom or your previous job to your future positions.

Hard Skills

Hard skills are skills that you have been formally taught. These skills include different software applications that you have learned in school or on the job. Think about the computer skills you have learned in school. There is a strong emphasis on excellent keyboarding skills. You have probably worked on timings throughout your school program, constantly pushing your words per minute while simultaneously trying to reduce the number of errors.

Think of the different software programs you have learned in school. You have spent a great deal of time on different software applications that can be applied in the law office. In family law, you have worked on DIVORCEmate. In real estate law, you have learned how to use Teraview and Conveyancer®. In estates, you have learned estate-a-base. You have also learned how to use PC Law™ for time management and billing purposes. You have learned how to draft court documents. You know how to docket your time and how important that is so that you can bill the client correctly. You have learned how to compose and set up a professional business/legal letter. Perhaps you have taken accounting or business courses and are also capable of applying these skills in a law firm.

Your hard skills are formal skills that you bring with you. They are things you can do.

List the different software applications you have learned to use:

_____

_____

_____

_____

_____

_____

_____

_____

List the different hard skills that you have learned. Which ones do you think are the most important?

_____

_____

_____

_____

_____

_____

_____

_____

_____

_____

_____

_____

_____

Soft Skills

Soft skills are interpersonal skills that no one has ever formally taught you. You naturally excel at them. Many of the skills that you have been using in part-time jobs are soft skills that are transferable to a full-time position.

Here are some examples of soft skills:

- Dealing well with people
- Being organized
- Managing your time effectively
- Paying attention to detail
- Working well on a team
- Working well independently
- Ability to multitask
- Being punctual
- Taking pride in the quality of work you produce

Think of your own soft skills that you bring to a job. In the space provided below, list your soft skills. Try to think of different soft skills that are not on the list above. Show at least 10 of your skills:

_____

_____

_____

_____

_____

_____

_____

Getting Organized for the Interview

There are many things that you need to do to be organized and ready for your interview. First, choose your interview clothes two to three days prior to your appointment. As discussed earlier in the workbook, ensure that your clothes are ironed and clean, with no holes, and your shoes are polished. This is being repeated here because it is crucial to make a good first impression. It is important that your image presents you in a professional manner as someone who can do the job.

If you do not have an appropriate outfit for the interview, make sure that you go shopping to purchase a professional business outfit that you can wear for interviews. These clothes do not need to be expensive. It is difficult financially when you are a student. You can buy pieces that look professional without spending a great deal of money.

Do not leave buying your interview outfit to the last minute. If you are having a hard time finding things you like that fit, it will add undue stress and pressure. Try to be organized and think ahead. More details on what to wear to the interview will be presented in a later chapter.

Print a hard copy of your resumé on a good bond paper. Make a hard copy of your reference page. Bring these to the interview in a large envelope or in a professional-looking portfolio. Have them ready so that you can pull them out easily at the beginning of the interview. You do not want to have to search for these papers in your purse or book bag. You also want them to be pristine copies, not folded or tattered. Know exactly where the documents are so that you can retrieve them instantly. Show potential employers how organized and professional you are.

During your interview, you may be asked about the kinds of documents and other work you have done in your program. It is fine to talk about drafting court documents, composing legal and business letters, the financial statements you have created in DIVORCEmate software, and the Transfer and Charge that you have created in Teraview software. It is even better to actually show samples of your work.

If you are showing copies of legal letters that you worked on in class, make sure that the copy you present to them has been marked, so that you know it is correct. Reprint the copy after the corrections have been made so that the final copy does not have any errors or red markings. The final work you present should be perfect. Avoid showing samples of your work that still have typos or red corrections that need to be redone.

If you have prepared a precedent binder it should hold all of your important document samples. Organize them in plastic protectors and dividers. When asked if you have ever drafted a Statement of Claim, instead of just saying that yes, you have, you can say yes and show a sample of the quality of your work. Showing your work is much more powerful and makes more of an impact than just talking about it. Use samples of your work as marketing tools to show off the quality of work that you are capable of doing.

Always take a pen (make sure it works!) and a pad of paper to the interview. Avoid taking notes during the interview, but if something comes, such as being given a website to check out, jot the information down for later reference. Being prepared with a pen and paper demonstrates that you are ready and interested in making any important notes, if necessary. This also shows that you are organized and thinking ahead. These are excellent qualities that anyone would want in their law clerk.

Prior to the interview, it is suggested that you complete a practice run to the office location. This will help you gauge how long it will take to get to the interview. Are you relying on public transit? Is there a subway or bus stop nearby? How much time should you allow for rush-hour traffic? How much time for public transit delays? What about delays due to road repairs? It is difficult to take all of the necessary factors into consideration but important to try to deal with as many as possible.

Your practice run will give you an opportunity to see exactly where the office is, if you are unfamiliar with that part of the city. It is also an opportunity for you to check out any coffee shops that are in the vicinity. If you arrive for the interview too early, you should not go in and just wait in the reception area for half an hour. That is much too much time spent waiting. Instead, always arrive early but go and have a coffee in a shop nearby. Take a few minutes there to gather your thoughts. Then go to the interview so that you arrive 10 minutes prior to the interview time.

Think of other things that you may need to do prior to your interview. Create a checklist of things that you must do to be organized and ready for your job interview. Put a check mark beside each item as it has been completed:

Things *Not* to Do

Just as it is important to do a number of things prior to the interview, it is also very important *not* to do certain things. While you are thinking of the important things to do, it will occur to you what should not be done.

The most important thing is to *never* be late for your interview. Being late could leave a potential employer wondering if this is a common occurrence for you.

Suppose you have done everything to prepare for the interview. The weekend before the interview, you have taken a trip to the office to see exactly where it is located. You have an idea of how much extra time it may take to allow for traffic delays. You feel you are prepared and ready to go.

Unfortunately, the unthinkable sometimes happens, like your alarm not going off. Things happen. Do the best that you can. If you see that you will definitely be late, *always* call ahead to let the person you are meeting know that you are running late and why. Have the courtesy to give the interviewer this information early so that he or she can plan time around you, if possible. You must respect the fact that the interviewer is very busy and might have scheduled back-to-back interviews. It may not be possible to meet with you later on that day. You will have to accept this. Being late could result in someone else getting the job instead of you. Try to avoid being late for the interview, at all costs.

Cellphones, which are an important part of our daily lives, are another topic of concern. Make sure that your cellphone *never* goes off during an interview! There is nothing more annoying to a potential employer than an applicant scrambling to find a cellphone in a purse or pocket and then trying to shut it off while apologizing profusely. Do not even put your phone on vibrate, thinking that only you know if it is going off. Others can hear or see your reaction and know that your phone is vibrating. Give the interviewer your undivided attention. Make sure that from your end, the interview is free from distractions. Always turn your phone off *before* walking into the office building for your interview.

Do not ask anyone to give you a ride home from the interview. If there is testing involved, or the interviewer is running late, an interview could sometimes take longer than thought. Do not have someone waiting for you in the reception area. This is not the professional image that you wish to convey. You do not want to keep glancing at your watch because you know that someone is waiting for you and the interview is taking longer than you expected. If you are old enough to go on a job interview, you are responsible enough to find your own way home.

For that same reason, you should not plan to meet people immediately after the interview. Again, make sure that you give the interview and the interviewer your undivided attention and concentrate on nothing else except what is happening in that room.

Give your interview the better part of your day, if possible. Allow yourself extra time to travel back and forth and also for the interview itself. The interview should be the most important event of the day. It could mean the difference of getting the job or not getting it.

Prepare yourself. Create a checklist here of some things that you do *not* want to do prior to an interview:

Use this space to make notes on what clothes you will wear and what you plan to bring with you to an interview:

_____

_____

_____

_____

_____

_____

_____

_____

_____

_____

_____

_____

_____

_____

_____

_____

_____

_____

_____

_____

_____

_____

_____

_____

_____

GETTING READY FOR WORK **A Career Preparation Workbook for Legal Students**

CHAPTER 3

The Interview

Things to Consider

Here you are at last! It has been a long road of preparation but you have been called for an interview. Finally! Now what will you do? There are so many things that are crucial for your consideration.

The first and most important thing is to be friendly and pleasant to everyone you encounter. You do not yet know who the players are. You might be sitting in reception waiting, when a man in jeans walks by, eating a hot dog and notices you. He asks who you are waiting for. Be pleasant and friendly. He could be the senior partner. You never know.

When you walk in and greet the receptionist, it is most important to be friendly and respectful. Treat every person you meet as you would treat the senior partner of the firm. In many offices, the receptionist is the person who will be asked by the HR people what you were like. If you are rude or abrupt to the receptionist, you may never get your foot in the door of that firm. Be professional.

When you approach the desk, if the receptionist is on the phone, wait until the call is finished. Then, smile and say who you are, who you are there to see, and the time of your appointment. Speak clearly so that the receptionist gets your name correct and can announce you accurately to the person you have the appointment with.

Waiting for Your Interview

Once you have announced yourself, it is time to take a seat and wait. Here is a list of things *not* to do while waiting to be called in for your interview.

- Do not text people on your cellphone.
- Do not check your messages on your cellphone.
- Do not make phone calls in the reception area.
- Do not check or apply your makeup.
- Do not comb your hair. Check your appearance in the restroom prior to walking into the reception area.
- Do not listen to your iPod and tune out to what is going on around you.
- Do not chew gum.

List other things you should *not* do while waiting for your interview:

_____

_____

_____

_____

_____

_____

_____

_____

It is perfectly acceptable to read a newspaper or flip through a magazine found in the reception area while you are waiting. Be aware of your surroundings and pay attention to the people who are walking through reception. This could be your future place of employment.

Anticipate the moment when you will be called in. What have you brought with you? You may have a portfolio and a file with a copy of your resumé. If you are a woman, you will probably have a purse. If you do have a number of items, the last thing you want to do is stand to meet the interviewer while juggling and trying to balance different things that you are carrying. You want to give the appearance of looking smooth. Make sure that when you stand to greet the interviewer, your right hand is free.

This raises the question, Should you shake hands with the interviewer? You are sitting in reception. A woman approaches and calls your name. You smile, stand, and walk toward her. Allow her to extend her hand to you. She will introduce herself. Say hello and shake her hand. Do not give a limp handshake. Do not squeeze her hand so hard that she loses all feeling for a week. When you shake hands, give a firm, confident handshake. Smile. Look the person in the eye and say, "It is very nice to meet you." Then follow the interviewer into the office where the interview will take place.

Testing

Law firms have very high standards regarding the quality of work and workplace skills. Employees need to have excellent skills and the quality of the work must be perfect. Since there are so many deadlines in this environment, the work must also be done quickly.

Testing can be an important part of the interview process. Many firms will do testing prior to talking to the candidate. Not all firms test but you should be prepared for this.

Large law firms have their own standard set of testing. They may test keyboarding speed, spelling, grammar, and proofreading. The testing process could take an hour. If you have questions about the testing, ask them at the start. For instance, how long will the testing take in total? This is a good question so that you can gauge your time accordingly and you have an idea before you begin. You also might wish to ask what you will be tested on.

Even interviews at smaller firms may have a keyboarding component for the candidate. It is important to see how many errors and at what rate the candidate can keyboard. With practice, your keyboarding skills will improve, so *keep practising.* This cannot be stressed enough. You will be working with colleagues who may be able to keyboard at 80 words per minute. If you are keyboarding at only 40 words per minute, it will take you twice as long to do the work. Practise constantly to improve your speed. Sending emails to friends or text messaging is not considered practising your keyboarding skills and it is not enough.

Never lie about your keyboarding speed to impress a potential employer. A lie could come back to bite you. Do not state your speed as 65 words per minute because that sounds good and you are hoping to be able to do that someday, maybe. If you have said that your speed is 65 words per minute and you are tested at 48 words per minute, you cannot just say that it is an "off day." Be realistic. If your keyboarding speed is only 48 words per minute, be honest about that. You can talk about this in a positive way by saying that you are working on improving your speed.

In an interview situation, your keyboarding test may take place at an available workspace in the middle of a busy, noisy office. This might not be an ideal situation. It might be difficult for you to concentrate. But concentrate, you must! See the important keyboarding tips below.

Tips for Your Best Keyboarding

Keyboarding during an interview can be very stressful. The testing environment may not be ideal. Here are 10 important tips to help you do your best keyboarding in a stressful interview situation:

1. Get comfortable in the chair. Adjust the height of the chair, if necessary so that you are in a comfortable keyboarding position.
2. Block out the noise and activity that is going on around you. This will not be easy. Phones might be ringing and people talking and laughing. Ignore them.
3. Concentrate only on what *you* are doing.
4. If possible, take a moment to read over what you will be keyboarding, this will help your fingers move faster because you will have an idea of what is coming to be typed.
5. Sit up straight in the chair with your feet flat on the floor and your back against the back of the chair.
6. Take a moment to position the keyboarding paper close to the monitor so that you can read it easily.
7. Do *not* take time to read the text word for word. Instead, read the words quickly so that your fingers can move speedily across the keyboard.
8. Take a moment before you start to flex your fingers, take a deep breath, and then begin.
9. If you make a mistake, *do not* stop. Just keep going.
10. Relax, concentrate, and type as quickly and accurately as you possibly can.

Create your own list of things that will help you to keyboard your best in an interview situation:

_____

_____

_____

_____

_____

_____

_____

_____

_____

_____

The Face-to-Face Interview

This is the moment you have been waiting for. You are sitting across the desk from the person interviewing you for a position in a law firm. Now what?

Remember _never_ put anything on the interviewer's desk. Hold the binder and portfolio on your lap. If you are asked for samples of the work you have produced, having your binder on your lap makes it easy for you to hand over. This is a much smoother transition to accessing your documents than bending to the floor to retrieve them.

Most people are nervous during an interview situation. Some people do not know what to do with their hands when they are nervous. Having placed a binder on your lap gives you something to hold on to and something to do with your hands. This will also prevent you from fidgeting.

When you are sitting across from the interviewer, it is important to listen intently to what is being said. Answer only the question being asked and don't ramble. It is easy to go off in different directions and go on and on. Stay focused and give articulate, well thought-out answers. Your answers should have a clear beginning and end. Keep your voice strong. Do not let it trail off at the end of your answer. Stay confident.

Just as important as not rambling is not giving yes, no, or one-word answers. The interview is your chance to show how articulate and thoughtful you are.

The interviewer wants to hear what you have to say. This is your opportunity to shine! Try to allow your personality and passion to show.

It is also important to give the interviewer your undivided attention. Do not glance out the window, around the room, or at your watch. Look the interviewer directly in the eye when speaking and listening. This shows that you are interested and focused on what is going on.

When possible, try to illustrate skills and strengths from a previous part-time job that can be applied to this full-time position. For example, if one of your strengths was dealing with customer complaints when you worked at a jean store, you will be able to use those strong people skills when dealing with unhappy clients in a law firm. Give examples of how you applied your skills when handling difficult situations. Highlight your skills and strengths. You are not bragging. It is necessary for the interviewer to be aware of areas where you excel.

At all times, remain respectful. It is also important to show that you respected people whom you have worked with in previous jobs. *Never* badmouth a former supervisor, employer, co-worker, or company. Saying negative things about a former employer only puts you in a bad light and suggests you may not work well with others. The interviewer may think that if you are putting down your last supervisor the same thing could happen when you leave this job. No matter how much you did not like someone or did not get along with a person in a previous position, always stay positive and respectful when discussing previous employment.

Do not be afraid to take a sip of water when you need it during an interview. Interviews can be quite stressful and can result in a dry mouth. Make sure that you are able to speak clearly. Sometimes taking a sip of water also allows you to stall for time when you are asked a question that you need to think about.

During the interview, be aware of your posture. Sit up straight and look alert. Be involved in what is going on. Stay in the present. Do not think about the assignment you have due or the laundry that has been piling up. Stay focused on the interview.

The interviewer wants to get to know you and how you think. Remember that. He or she wants you to be successful. Try to be as articulate as possible in your answers. Allow your enthusiasm, commitment, and passion to shine. Highlight your skills and abilities. Let the interviewer know what contributions you can make to the firm.

The interview is also your opportunity to learn about this firm. Ask intelligent questions about the firm so that you are able to judge whether you could see yourself working there. This is your opportunity to see if the firm's culture is a good match for you as a person. If you are interested in the position and would love to work at the firm, do not be afraid to say so. The interview is your opportunity to show what you can contribute. Participate in it with confidence. Act self-assured with head held high and be convinced that you will give the best interview possible.

Never give an answer because you think it is what the interviewer wants to hear. Just be yourself! Set realistic goals so that, if you are asked, you can truly tell the interviewer where you see yourself in the future. In preparation for the day ahead, arrange to have a calm night before the day of the interview.

Do's and Don'ts During an Interview

Things you should do in an interview:

- Make eye contact with the interviewer.
- Give the interviewer 100 percent of your undivided attention.
- Be and look interested during the interview.
- Smile when it is appropriate.
- Answer only the question being asked with a proper beginning and ending to your answer. Emphasize how important skills you have demonstrated can be applied to this position.
- Keep your voice strong and confident.
- Be positive, pleasant, friendly, and respectful.
- Be honest.
- Take a bottle of water with you in case you have a dry mouth—it is important that you are able to express yourself properly.
- Offer examples of how you have handled situations in the past.
- When discussing former employers, firms, companies, and colleagues, always remain positive.
- Use this as your opportunity to show how capable you are by highlighting your strengths.
- Try to let your personality shine through.
- Show interest in the interview and enthusiasm for the job.

- Sit up straight and look confident.
- Ask interesting questions about the position and intelligent questions about the firm.
- If there is an area where you are weak, explain that you are working on it.
- Act as you would if you already had the job without giving the impression of arrogance.
- Explain what *you* can do for *them*.
- When the interview is complete, stand, smile, give the interviewer a firm handshake, and say that it was a pleasure to meet him or her. If you are truly interested in the position, don't be afraid to say so.

Things you should not do in an interview:

- Do not glance around the room or look out the window when talking or being asked a question.
- Do not answer questions with a yes, or no, or one-word answers.
- Do not try to be humorous. What you think is funny, others may not.
- Do not say you would like to work there to gain more experience for *you*.
- Do not ask about salary.
- Do not ask about holiday time or sick days.
- Do not let your answers ramble on and on with no direction.
- Do not let your voice trail off at the end of an answer.
- Do not fidget.
- When asked if you have any questions, do not say no. That makes you look like you are not interested.
- Do not glance at your watch during the interview.
- Do not say anything negative about former employers.
- If you are unsure how to answer a question, do not just stare at the interviewer while you are trying to think of a good answer. Ask to come back to the question.
- If you truly do not know the answer, do not try to "fake" it.
- Do not give an answer because you think it is what the interviewer "wants" to hear.
- Do not try to make your previous jobs or tasks sound more important or responsible than they were.
- Do not slouch or sit slumped in the chair.
- Do not chew gum during the interview.
- Never exaggerate when talking about your skills.
- Do not be arrogant.
- Do not interrupt while the interviewer is speaking.

List your own <u>things you should do</u> in an interview:

_____

_____

_____

_____

_____

_____

_____

_____

_____

List your own <u>things you should not do</u> in an interview:

_____

_____

_____

_____

_____

_____

_____

_____

_____

_____

_____

After the Interview

The interview is over and you are relieved. You are hoping that it went well. Now, you can only sit and wait to hear from the firm. An important follow-up is to send a thank-you note to the person who interviewed you. It could be an email, but a short letter may be even more impressive. Make sure that you have the correct name and title of the person who interviewed you.

Your thank-you note should be short and to the point. Thank the interviewer for taking the time to see you. Let the interviewer know that you enjoyed the meeting and that you are looking forward to hearing from the firm in the near future. Be polite. Make sure that you proofread the note before sending it.

If you are sending an email, make sure that the subject line pertains to the body of the email. Never use slang in your email such as "Hey." Keep your email professional. Make sure that the spelling, grammar, and sentence structure are perfect. If you are sending a thank you with typos or errors, you are leaving a negative lasting impression. That is something that you do not want to do.

A thank-you note is not mandatory, but it could make a difference as to whether or not you get a positive response from your interview.

CHAPTER 4

Expectations of a Law Firm

Professionalism and Attitude

You are thrilled. You got the job! You are sure that you will dazzle them with your skills and abilities and before long, you will be a manager. Right? Perhaps, perhaps not. Not yet, at least. Remember that it is necessary to pay your dues. Have realistic expectations. No one starts at the top.

If working in a large firm is your goal, expect to be hired into a junior position. You have a good education, you may have excellent skills but you need to get your foot in the door before you can show off what you can do.

Senior law clerks and lawyers may not trust you with their work right away. They are very protective of their files, work, and clients. An excellent quality of work is of the utmost importance. They may give you a little job, such as typing a letter, to see how you handle it. If you do a good job on that, you might get more work. No matter how small the task, do the best job that you can do. No assignment is too small and no task is too menial. If it is filing, treat it as a learning experience. See how their filing system is set up. If it is a letter you are asked to do, always make sure you proofread it and it is *perfect* before you give it back for a signature. If you want them to trust you, show them that you are capable of high-quality work in a timely manner. As you successfully meet the expectations of the firm, more challenging work may be given to you. To get to the point where you are assigned the type of work you want, you must show them that you are conscientious and efficient.

Slowly, over time, their trust in your work will build once you prove to them that the quality of your work is consistently excellent.

There are differences between working in a large firm and working in a smaller firm. In a large firm, you might only work on one small part of a file or one thing and then the file is passed to another clerk to take it from there. You may only be in a typing pool. Remember that you must pay your dues and prove what you are capable of doing before people will give you a chance to move on. If the quality of your work is consistently good, people will notice.

In a smaller firm, things are different. There is a greater chance for more hands-on work right away. Since there are fewer people to do the work, you may find yourself dealing with clients right away and working through an entire file.

Always remember that the firm has high expectations that require perfection for any work you do. The work cannot just be pretty good. You are working in a law firm. The work must be perfect!

Professionalism

Large and small law firms have one thing in common: they are paying you to do a job perfectly. That is what they expect of you. You are there to work. It is of course important to be friendly with your co-workers. However, the firm also wants to see you take a serious interest in the work at hand.

Employers frown upon staff taking time out to text message, listen to an iPod, go on MSN, Hotmail, Facebook, or Twitter while at work. These activities might be a part of your regular life, but at work these things are viewed as time taken away from the work you are being paid to do. Do not think that you can sneak these things in and if they are minimized at the bottom of your screen, no one will notice. You are only fooling yourself. People will notice. You want to give a professional impression to your co-workers and employers. Show them that you are hard working, committed, and professional. Show them that you have a mature attitude about work and take it seriously. When it comes time for promotions, people will notice if you are doing all of the right things. Concentrate on your work. Stay away from distractions.

Punctuality

The importance of punctuality is crucial. You may think no one will notice if you slip in five minutes late, or apologize with an excuse that the buses were late again or that traffic was heavy, but someone will. Allow extra time for rush-hour traffic and delays. Be at your desk 10 to 15 minutes prior to your starting time. Turn on your computer, get a coffee, and be back at your desk ready to work when you are supposed to be. The same goes for coffee breaks. If you are given a 10-minute coffee break, that does not mean that you return to your desk in 11 minutes or 20. It means you are back in 10 minutes. Be aware of your time. Being punctual is part of being professional.

Attitude

The importance of attitude cannot be stressed enough. A good attitude is everything. Show that you have a positive attitude, no matter what task you are given. Use each task, no matter how mundane, as a learning experience. If you are asked to photocopy a file, learn how their files are set up, what filing system they use, and how they set up their letters in the file. Use every task to try to make yourself a more valuable member of the team and to get to know the ins and outs of the firm.

Be a team player. If you have completed all of your work, do not just sit and wait for someone to assign you something. Walk around and *ask* if there is anything you can help with. Offer your help to others who are swamped with work. Show your co-worker and your manager that you are an eager part of the team. Show them that you are interested in learning and committed to doing a good job. Become an important part of the team. There may come a time when you are the busy one in need of help.

Ask Questions

If you have been given an assignment but are unclear as to exactly what it is you are supposed to do, ask questions for clarification. Do not be afraid that you are asking a "dumb" question. There is no such thing. There is nothing worse than *thinking* you understand, spending a couple of hours working on the task, and then finding out that it was done incorrectly and must be completely redone. You have not only wasted valuable time and money but you have now created a situation where people may have lost confidence in your ability.

Do not be afraid to repeat the instructions to ensure that they are correct. "So you would like me to send a letter to this client at his business address and include a copy of the document we received from the other side." Clarify your instructions prior to starting work on the task, not after it has been completed.

Proofread Your Work

You must *always* proofread your work. This is one of the most important things you can do. It does not matter how rushed the job is. It does not matter how stressed or busy you are. Take the time to proofread your work before it is checked by your supervisor and before it is sent to the client. This cannot be stressed enough. Think of how you would feel as a client, receiving a document or letter from your law firm with typographical errors or your name spelled incorrectly. Does that instill confidence in the firm's ability? Or does it make you want to switch to a law firm that can spell their clients' names correctly?

Be Prepared

When your lawyer calls you into the office to tell you something, always go in prepared. Take a pad of paper and pen with you. Take notes on the things that you are being given to do. The lawyer may call you in for one thing and then think of 10 other things for you to do. You cannot possibly remember everything. You will remember, however, if you are organized.

Office Politics

Stay away from gossip and office politics. It might be interesting to hear, but will it help you to do a better job? No. You are there to work, so don't jeopardize that. Keep your nose clean. Do not get involved. Do not talk about or spread rumours about people. Keep your head down and mind your own business. You are there to work, so work.

Confidentiality

When you are working in a law firm, you are dealing with the most private and confidential aspects of people's lives. It could be a divorce, a criminal conviction, a will, a real estate transaction. Whatever it is, you are privy to information that is of a confidential nature. This trust can never be violated.

It is not to be used as a topic for interesting conversation with your friends, co-workers, family or as gossip on the public transit at night. The information that your clients trust you with must at all times remain confidential.

Social Networking Sites and Privacy

Do not assume that others cannot access your personal email. Always be very careful about what you write in your emails at the office. *Never* bad-mouth the firm, a boss, or a co-worker in your emails. Be careful about which Internet sites you visit from the office. Most offices have IT staff or security staff that have the capabilities of monitoring your email and which Internet sites you visit. Do not put yourself in a position where your integrity is in question because you were doing something that you thought was "private."

Another area that you should be aware of is your Facebook page. It has become standard practice for some firms and companies to check the Facebook page of staff or potential staff. There is a way to make your Facebook page private so only friends can see it, however, IT can easily get into that. Make sure that the pictures you post on Facebook are not showing you wildly partying on your last holiday if you want to work for a conservative law firm.

Some job offers have been contingent on the candidate removing his or her Facebook account because it was not the image of employees that the firm wanted to project.

Networking

Whether you are aware of it or not, everything you do is an opportunity for networking. The legal community is very small and connected. You are constantly meeting and dealing with people who know lawyers. At any given time, some of those lawyers are looking to hire staff.

Get out there and get involved. Volunteer your time! Join sports groups and clubs. Join professional associations and organizations. Meet people. Look at the people with whom you work or went to school. They are all valuable networking connections. They could all lead you to future employment opportunities.

Enhance Your Image Exercise

List five things you can do to enhance your professional image in the workplace and indicate why these things are important:

What you can do	Why this is important
1.	
2.	
3.	
4.	
5.	

Notes and Exercises

Looking at Yourself

List any organizations to which you belong.

_____

_____

_____

_____

_____

_____

_____

_____

List any volunteer work that you have done.

_____

_____

_____

_____

_____

_____

_____

_____

List any important achievements, which should include awards or certificates that you have earned.

_____

_____

_____

_____

_____

_____

_____

_____

_____

Think about your goals and list them here. What would you like to be doing in one year? in two years? in five years? Include what you will have to do to realize them.

_____

_____

_____

_____

_____

_____

_____

_____

_____

_____

_____

Prepare a list of adjectives that describe your attitude toward work. Developing this list will help clarify and reinforce your strengths. It will also help you to "sell" yourself to potential employers in a professional and positive light.

_____

_____

_____

_____

_____

_____

_____

_____

_____

_____

Give examples of situations where you have demonstrated the strengths listed above.

_____

_____

_____

_____

_____

_____

_____

_____

_____

_____

_____

Test Your Legal Knowledge

How much do you know about the legal profession? Do you know the players? Do you know the organizations? Are you familiar with the legal software? Try the following exercise to test your knowledge about various people and organizations within the legal community.

Legal Knowledge Exercise

You may have to do some research to answer the questions below.

What is the purpose of the Law Society of Upper Canada?

_____

_____

_____

The current Chief Justice of Canada is

_____

The current Chief Justice of Ontario is

_____

The Chief Justice of Ontario presides over which court?

_____

The previous Chief Justice of Ontario is

_____

When addressing a letter to the Chief Justice of Ontario, what is the correct title that should be used?

_____

_____

How do you address a Judge?

_____

What is the difference between a Judge and a Justice of the Peace?

_____

Who is the Attorney General of Ontario?

_____

What is the correct title when addressing a letter to the Attorney General of Ontario?

_____

_____

What is the complete formal name for OJEN?

_____

Who started OJEN?

_____

What is the purpose of OJEN?

_____

_____

_____

What is the full formal name of AIDWYC?

_____

_____

What is the purpose of AIDWYC?

_____

_____

_____

_____

Name two famous cases handled by AIDWYC.

1. _____

_____

2. _____

_____

What is the purpose of the Canadian Civil Liberties Association?

_____

_____

_____

List other important legal organizations and identify their purpose.

_____

_____

_____

_____

_____

Why is Teraview important for real estate law in Ontario?

_____

_____

_____

What is PC Law™ used for in a law office?

_____

_____

_____

_____

Why is DIVORCEmate software used in a law firm?

_____

_____

_____

Identify other legal software applications for other areas of law. Why is it important to know how to use these in a law office? Include the area of law where they would be used.

1. _____

_____

_____

2. _____

_____

_____

3. _____

_____

_____

4. _____

_____

_____

5. _____

_____

_____

Test Your Proofreading, Grammar, and Spelling Skills

The importance of proofreading and checking your work cannot be stressed enough. When working in law, your work must not only be good, it *must* be perfect. Working under pressure, deadlines, and time constraints are not excuses for errors. You must proofread for all mistakes, including spelling, punctuation, typos, capitalization, and proper usage of words. You must always take the time to check and recheck your work. You must always proofread your work thoroughly. If you are not committed to painstakingly proofreading every character in every sentence of every letter or document you produce, law is not for you. For a successful career in law, you must be dedicated to high-quality work and committed to achieving a higher standard of performance. Lawyers have extremely high expectations about how their documents and letters should look. They are sticklers for detail and demand top-quality work and perfection. If you wish to be successful in this profession, these must be your standards as well.

Proofreading, Grammar, and Spelling Exercises

The following exercises have been designed to test your proofreading, grammar, and spelling skills. Read through each exercise carefully before you begin.

Exercise 1

Circle the incorrect word and write the correct word at the end of that line:

	Circle the incorrect word	Correct the word
1	There trail date is set for Feburary 10th, next year.	
2	I here the Judge is very tough.	
3	I no someone who was charged in a similiar case and one.	
4	There are to defendents in this case who	
5	use to be good friends.	
6	There no longer speeking.	
7	i no this is very stressful four the families involved.	
8	Luckily, they have a very good lowyer.	
9	To many young people are making bad choices and	
10	not thinking about there future.	
11	When will they realize that a education is so important	
12	and can change your live?	

How many errors did you find?

Exercise 2

Circle the incorrect word and write the correct word at the end of that line:

	Circle the incorrect word	Correct the word
1	Alot of the backlog in our criminal court system today	
2	is due to pety crime comitted by board youth.	
3	The court calenders are filled with trials.	
4	It is upsetting that so many at risk youths do not seam	
5	to have a conscious when it comes to commiting crimes.	
6	The courts are not able to accomodeate all of the cases	
7	brought be for them in a timely fashion.	
8	It is not acceptible that cases are thrown out	
9	because it took to long to come to trial.	
10	This seems to be a common occurance and	
11	somthing needs to be done to change things.	
12	More programs need to be in place so that trubbled youth	
13	can funnel there energy and time in a positive way.	
14	It is not to late.	
15	We can still make a diffrence in the lives of many people.	
16	We need perserverence by a commited group of people	
17	too make things change.	
18	We can definately do this!	

How many errors did you find?

_____

Exercise 3

Select the correct word for each sentence. Write it in the blank provided.

1. _____ mother was so happy to see them.
   (There/Their/They're)

2. There were _____ many things to do in the morning.
   (to/two/too)

3. _____ Honour, that is the way things happened.
   (You're/Your)

4. It is a pleasure to _____ you.
   (meet/meat)

5. She has to get _____ work on time.
   (to/two/too)

6. _____ a shame that more cannot be done.
   (Its'/It's/Its)

7. The argument was over the _____ of the thing.
   (principal/principle)

8. The choice was between _____ different issues.
   (two/too/to)

9. _____ having a party this Saturday night.
   (Their/There/They're)

10. _____ are the new clothes that you want to _____ ?
    (Where/Wear)   (where/wear)

Use the space below to list the words that you have difficulty with in a sentence. Make notes to remind you how to use the words properly.

Test Your Keyboarding Skills

You are employed as a law clerk with the firm of Wiley, Riley, and Smiley. Your boss, Richard Wiley, has asked that you type a letter that he has handwritten. The address of your firm is 393 Bay Street, Suite 3200, Toronto, ON M5H 3R3. The letter is going to your client, Harold Smithers, who resides at 2793 Old Orchard Park, Toronto ON M5T 3M3.

Keyboarding Exercise

Create a proper legal letter on firm letterhead that will be ready for Mr. Wiley to sign. Add a footer that includes your name. Print a copy of the completed letter and include it in the Additional Notes section of this workbook.

We are enclosing the agreement as discussed in our telephone conversation yesterday. There have been a few changes in particular to paragraphs 3 and 4 that you should be aware of. These changes do not have an impact on the overall agreement.
However make sure that you read them carefully and are comfortable with them.

If you have any questions, do not hesitate to contact me. Looking forward to our next golf game.

Answer Keys

Legal Knowledge Exercise

Question	Answer
What is the purpose of the Law Society of Upper Canada?	The Law Society of Upper Canada governs legal services providers in the public interest by ensuring that the people of Ontario are served by lawyers and paralegals who meet high standards of learning, competence, and professional conduct.
The current Chief Justice of Canada is	The Right Honourable Beverley McLachlin
The current Chief Justice of Ontario is	The Honourable Warren K. Winkler
The Chief Justice of Ontario presides over which court?	Court of Appeal for Ontario
The previous Chief Justice of Ontario is	The Honourable R. Roy McMurtry
When addressing a letter to the Chief Justice of Ontario, what is the correct title that should be used?	The Honourable Warren K. Winkler Chief Justice of Ontario Address
How do you address a Judge?	• In conversation: Your Honour • Salutation in a letter: Dear Mr./Madam Justice:
What is the difference between a Judge and a Justice of the Peace?	• Justices of the Peace are restricted in the types of matters (both area of law, type of hearing) they can adjudicate, and sit only on the Ontario Court of Justice. Judges are not restricted in the type of matter they can adjudicate, and can preside over any level of court to which they are appointed. • A Judge is a lawyer; a Justice of the Peace does not have to be a lawyer.

Who is the Attorney General of Ontario?	The Honourable Chris Bentley
What is the correct title when addressing a letter to the Attorney General of Ontario?	The Hon. Chris Bentley Attorney General of Ontario
What is the complete formal name for OJEN?	Ontario Justice Education Network
Who started OJEN?	Then Chief Justice of Ontario Roy McMurtry, then Chief Justice of the Superior Court of Justice Patrick LeSage, and then Chief Justice of the Ontario Court of Justice Brian W. Lennox. In 2000 they established the Public Legal Education Task Force to explore ways of increasing the public's understanding of the role of judges and the operation of our legal system.
What is the purpose of OJEN?	To increase the public's understanding of the role of judges and the operation of our legal system.
What is the full formal name of AIDWYC?	Association in Defence of the Wrongfully Convicted
What is the purpose of AIDWYC?	1. To eradicate the conditions that can cause miscarriages of justice. 2. To participate in the review and, where warranted, correction of wrongful convictions.
Name two famous cases handled by AIDWYC.	• William Mullins-Johnson • Robert Baltovich
What is the purpose of the Canadian Civil Liberties Association?	To promote respect for and observance of fundamental human rights and civil liberties, and to defend and ensure the protection and full exercise of those rights and liberties.
List other important legal organizations and identify their purpose.	• Pro Bono Law Ontario promotes access to justice in Ontario by creating and promoting opportunities for lawyers to provide pro bono (free) legal services to persons of limited means. • CLEONet is a website of legal information for community workers and advocates who work with low-income and disadvantaged communities, to help such workers help their clients exercise their rights.

Why is Teraview important for real estate law in Ontario?	Teraview is a mandatory software for lawyers who practise real estate law in Ontario. The software is used for searching title, creating electronic instruments, and registering documents for real estate transactions.
What is PC Law™ used for in a law office?	PC Law™ is used to docket time spent on individual files, and to record disbursements incurred on behalf of clients, for the purpose of billing.
Why is DIVORCEmate software used in a law firm?	Depending on the DIVORCEmate product, it can be used to to generate family law forms (from precedents) based on client information, calculate child support and spousal support, etc.
Identify other legal software applications for other areas of law. Why is it important to know how to use these in a law office? Include the area of law where they would be used.	• Conveyancer: used in real estate law • estate-a-base: used in estate law • ACL: used in litigation law • Fast Company: used in corporate law

Proofreading, Grammar, and Spelling Exercises

Exercise 1

Corrections for the 20 errors in this exercise are shown below.

	Circle the incorrect word	Correct the word
1	There trail date is set for Feburary 10th, next year.	Their/trial/February
2	I here the Judge is very tough.	hear
3	I no someone who was charged in a similiar case and one.	know/similar/won
4	There are to defendents in this case who	two/defendants
5	use to be good friends.	used
6	There no longer speeking.	They are/speaking
7	i no this is very stressful four the families involved.	I/know/for
8	Luckily, they have a very good lowyer.	lawyer
9	To many young people are making bad choices and	Too
10	not thinking about there future.	their
11	When will they realize that a education is so important	an
12	and can change your live?	life

Exercise 2

Corrections for the 22 errors in this exercise are shown below.

	Circle the incorrect word	Correct the word
1	(Alot)of the backlog in our criminal court system today	A lot
2	is due to(pety)crime(comitted)by(board)youth.	petty/committed/bored
3	The court(calenders)are filled with trials.	calendars
4	It is upsetting that so many at risk youths do not(seam)	seem
5	to have a(conscious)when it comes to(commiting)crimes.	conscience/committing
6	The courts are not able to(accomodeate)all of the cases	accommodate
7	brought(be for)them in a timely fashion.	before
8	It is not(acceptible)that cases are thrown out	acceptable
9	because it took(to)long to come to trial.	too
10	This seems to be a common(occurance)and	occurrence
11	(somthing)needs to be done to change things.	something
12	More programs need to be in place so that(trubbled)youth	troubled
13	can funnel(there)energy and time in a positive way.	their
14	It is not(to)late.	too
15	We can still make a(diffrence)in the lives of many people.	difference
16	We need(perserverence)by a(commited)group of people	perseverance/committed
17	(too)make things change.	to
18	We can(definately)do this!	definitely

Exercise 3

The correct answers are shown in boldface below.

1. **Their** mother was so happy to see them.
2. There were **too** many things to do in the morning.
3. **Your** Honour, that is the way things happened.
4. It is a pleasure to **meet** you.
5. She has to get **to** work on time.
6. **It's** a shame that more cannot be done.
7. The argument was over the **principle** of the thing.
8. The choice was between **two** different issues.
9. **They're** having a party this Saturday night.
10. **Where** are the new clothes that you want to **wear**?

Websites and Organizations of Interest

Career Websites

Here are some suggested important websites that might be helpful in assisting you in your job search. Some are legal websites, some are not.

- College Career website at Seneca College: https://www.senecacareerlink.com/careerlink
- Institute of Law Clerks of Ontario (ILCO): http://www.ilco.on.ca
- Ontario Public Service Careers: http://www.gojobs.gov.on.ca/Search.aspx
- Public Service Commission of Canada/Careers in the federal Public Service: http://jobs-emplois.gc.ca
- Workopolis: http://www.workopolis.com
- Monster: http://www.monster.ca
- Charity Village (for nonprofit sector): http://www.charityvillage.com
- Check the websites of individual law firms of interest
- Total legal jobs: http://www.totallegaljobs.ca
- Indeed: http://www.indeed.ca
- Careerbuilder: http://www.careerbuilder.ca

Important Legal Organizations

Here is a list of some important legal organizations that you should be aware of. You may wish to investigate some of these further.

- Law Society of Upper Canada (LSUC)
- Criminal Lawyers' Association (CLA)
- Canadian Civil Liberties Association (CCLA)
- Canadian Civil Liberties Education Trust (CCLET)
- Ontario Justice Education Network (OJEN)
- Association in Defence of the Wrongly Convicted (AIDWYC)
- Legal Aid Ontario (LAO)
- Canadian Bar Association (CBA)
- Ontario Bar Association (OBA)
- Ombudsman of Ontario
- Community Legal Education Ontario (CLEO)
- Association of Community Legal Clinics of Ontario
- Ontario Federation of Indian Friendship Centres (OFIFC)
- Ontario Council of Agencies Serving Immigrants (OCASI)
- Pro Bono Law Ontario (PBLO)

Professional Associations

Here is a list of some important professional legal associations. You may consider becoming a member of one or more of these organizations. Be aware that this is not a complete listing of all legal associations for law clerks, legal assistants, and paralegals.

- Institute of Law Clerks of Ontario (ILCO)
- Law Office Management Association (TLOMA)
- International Paralegal Management Association (IPMA)
- Association of Canadian Court Administrators (ACCA)
- Canadian Association of Paralegals (CAP)
- Association for Legal Professionals (NALS)
- National Federation of Paralegal Associations (NFPA)
- Association of Legal Administrators (ALA)
- Professional Paralegal Society of Ontario (PSO)
- Ontario Trial Lawyers Association (OTLA)—Law Clerk Section

Exercises

Select three career websites from those listed on page 73. Research a minimum of three job postings for each of the websites selected. Show the information here, giving full details of the websites and the job postings.

1. _____

_____

_____

_____

_____

_____

_____

_____

_____

_____

2. _____

_____

_____

_____

_____

_____

_____

_____

_____

_____

_____

3.

_____

_____

_____

_____

_____

_____

_____

_____

_____

_____

_____

_____

List other websites that will be useful to help you in your job search.

_____

_____

_____

_____

_____

_____

_____

_____

_____

_____

_____

_____

Select three of the legal organizations shown on page 74. Research and give details of each organization.

1.
\
\
\
\
\
\
\
\
\
\
\
\
\
\

2.
\
\
\
\
\
\
\
\
\
\
\
\
\
\
\
\
\

3. _____

_____

_____

_____

_____

_____

_____

_____

_____

_____

Identify three additional legal organizations of interest to you that are not listed above and explain their appeal.

1. _____

_____

_____

_____

_____

_____

_____

_____

_____

2. _____

_____

_____

_____

_____

_____

_____

_____

_____

_____

_____

_____

3. _____

_____

_____

_____

_____

_____

_____

_____

_____

_____

_____

_____

_____

Select two professional associations listed on page 74 that are of interest to you. Research the associations and provide details of each.

1. _____

_____

_____

_____

_____

_____

_____

_____

2. _____

_____

_____

_____

_____

_____

_____

_____

_____

Identify other professional organizations of interest to you that are not listed above and explain their appeal.

_____

_____

_____

_____

_____

_____

_____

_____

_____

Additional Notes

_____

_____

_____

_____

_____

_____

_____

_____

_____

_____

_____

The key to a successful future depends on *you*. Good luck!